CW00421211

Rambling Basics: Your Beginners Guide

ISBN-13: 978-1481111324
ISBN-10: 1481111329

Copyright Notice

RAMBLING BASICS: YOUR BEGINNERS GUIDE

Peter Deltrin

For ramblers everywhere...

Contents

The History of Rambling

Rambling started growing in popularity during the mid-1800s, particularly in the United Kingdom's northern cities. The interest in this outdoor activity is believed to have arisen because of the cramped and dirty living conditions at the time.

People naturally began to have a desire to explore the open spaces in the countryside. The problem was that a vast majority of the open lands were privately-owned and closed to the public.

Although paths were made around the Kinder Scout plateau, no path existed for people who wanted to cross it.

And gamekeepers guarded the land very closely to make sure no one made the mistake of straying from the footpaths.

Rambling clubs were first established in the late 1800s and these clubs started a long campaign to have greater access to those stretches of moorland they've long wanted to explore.

The Access to Mountains Bill was drafted and presented to Parliament a total of 18 times from 1884 to 1932.

However, the Bill failed to pass every single time. And though the rambling clubs also negotiated with individual landowners for access to their lands, most of these landowners persisted in denying them access, especially since they knew the law was in their favour.

By the year 1932, many young ramblers have become so frustrated by the failures suffered in the legal battles.

As a result, they decided to draw attention to their cause in a completely different way.

The Rambler's Right Movement and the British Workers Sports Federation sent out invitations to all ramblers to take part in a mass trespass right on Kinder Scout.

They believed the gamekeepers would never be able to keep them out if they went there in a huge number.

True enough, they were successfully able to ramble through Kinder Scout on April 24, 1932.

This resulted in the arrest of six men and the conviction of five for breach of the peace and unlawful assembly.

People differed in opinion as regards what the trespass was able to achieve.

There are those who believe it successfully brought attention to their plight, but there are also those who feared that it would hurt whatever progress they've had so far in terms of gaining greater access. In truth, there were no major changes immediately after that event.

The most significant development occurred in 1939, when the Mountain Access Bill finally won in Parliament.

World War II, however, caused a delay in the enactment of the bill and it was only in 1949 that the first national park was created as a result of the National Park Act.

This finally allowed ramblers to traverse the moorland.

For many years, though, most of the other lands in the area that weren't part of the Peak District were still inaccessible to ramblers.

Only after the Countryside and Rights of Way Act was passed in the year 2000 were a lot of the ramblers' goals finally achieved.

It may have taken 116 years to achieve their goals, but the ramblers of today are surely glad that the efforts of those who came before them have finally paid off.

A Quick Overview

Rambling is often considered as the United Kingdom's largest recreational activity. It has also become quite popular in many other parts of the world.

There are people who call it a participation sport. As compared to other sports, it is considerably gentler and involves much less impact on your body.

The benefits and pleasures you get from it, however, are numerous and very significant.

Even the shortest rambling trips can effectively refresh and invigorate you.

And as you move on to more challenging rambling adventures, you'll surely feel exhilarated and experience a sense of achievement even when you're physically exhausted.

One of the best things about a sport such as rambling is that just about everybody can engage in it. You can do it for just a few hours or for a couple of days, depending on your fitness and skill level.

As a beginner, it may be a good idea for you to go on rambling adventures in nearby areas.

You'd also do well to choose trails that aren't very challenging or mountainous while you're still building your endurance and fitness level for the sport.

The best trails to choose for your first few rambling adventures are those that simply allow you to enjoy the wonders of nature without too much exertion.

If you feel like you need a break from a stressful work atmosphere, then you could choose to go on a solo rambling adventure to unwind.

Another option would be for you to spend a weekend rambling trip bonding with family and friends. If you choose to join a rambling club, then a rambling trip may even be an excellent way to meet some new friends and strengthen old friendships.

The good news is that you can continue to engage in rambling activities even as you grow old. Though you may no longer be able to conquer long and arduous trails or walk as fast as when you were young, but that doesn't really matter.

Rambling is a personal experience and you do it only for your own enjoyment, rather than to impress other people.

The military often refers to rambling as tabbling or yomping. Some people also simply call it walking or hiking. Basically, it simply involves the act of putting one of your feet in front of the other.

From conquering the simpler trails in rambling, you can gradually move on to more challenging ones.

Someday, you may even choose to engage in even more exciting activities where you use not only your feet, but also your hands. These activities include scrambling and rock climbing.

If you have no previous experience in hiking or rambling and you're wondering how to get started in this outdoor adventure, it's easy, actually.

You could look for a family member or friend who has been engaged in the activity before and ask to join him on his next adventure.

Another option would be for you to join a rambling club where you'll learn the basics of the sport and get to join the group on their rambling trips. Ramble on!

What to Love about Rambling

Rambling has become a very popular activity in many parts of the world, particularly in Europe.

There are several reasons why people choose to engage in this activity and reasons why it would be a good idea for you to start rambling as well.

Here are some of the things you just have to love about this outdoor adventure called rambling:

1. Rambling is something that has been done by people for hundreds of years. In fact, it has been done possibly since the beginning of time. You may call it trekking, hiking, or bushwalking depending on what part of the world you live in. What remains the same is that it's a popular and completely natural activity.

2. Rambling can be done by people regardless of their age. That's because you can walk at your own pace and walk only for as long as you want. It's a personal experience so you get to plan your own trip.

3. Rambling can be the perfect activity to engage in if you want to bond with family and friends. It's also a good way for making new friends. Even if you choose not to join a rambling club, you still get the chance to meet other ramblers along the trail.

4. Rambling is an excellent form of exercise. It gives you the opportunity to breathe in fresh air, thus refreshing your lungs and enhancing your cardiovascular health in the process. It helps lower your blood cholesterol levels, increase bone density, and relieves you of stress. It also helps strengthen your sense of balance and allows you to get rid of excess body fat.

5. Rambling gives you the opportunity to explore nature and be amazed at all the wonders it has to offer. As you get awed by nature's beauty, your mind is effectively taken off of the pressures and stresses of your daily routines.

6. As long as you follow the principle of leaving no trace, rambling can also be the most environment-friendly sport. That's because this principle requires you to leave the trail much better than you found it.

7. You can go rambling even with just a few pieces of equipment. Basically, you just need the right clothing, a pair of top-quality boots, and water. If you plan to follow a hilly trail, then you also need a pair of walking poles to keep your knees strong and safe from injury.

8. You don't have to go far to enjoy rambling. There's sure to be a trail somewhere near you for a quick weekend getaway.

9. It's free! Well, practically free, since you'll only be spending money on your gear and transportation from your house to the head of the trail.

Considering all of the above, there's really no good reason for you not to try this outdoor adventure, is there?

There isn't that many activities that provide you with a considerable number of health and fitness benefits without involving too much cost.

What to Bring While Rambling

The things you need to bring on a rambling adventure trip depend in part on the trail you plan to traverse.

After all, you'll hardly need to bring a sleeping bag or tent if you're just going to follow a short trail that takes only a few hours to complete.

If, however, you're planning to follow a longer route that may take a few days to complete, then you'll definitely have to bring more things.

This is especially true since the weather may change unexpectedly while you're on the trail and that's something you'll have to be prepared for.

Don't be overconfident when you experience good weather in the valley, as wind levels and temperatures are likely to change just several hundred metres above.

Here's a list of the most basic items you'll have to bring with you on a rambling trip:

1. Food and water that's enough for the entire duration of your trip. If you're not quite sure how much you'll need, bring a bit more than the amount you think you'll need just to be on the safe side.

   You'd also do well to bring some high-energy food, which can be very useful in case you run out of food.

2. Appropriate clothing for the climate and environment you'll be going to. If you're likely to be crossing streams along the way, then you should definitely bring some extra dry clothes. In fact, it's a good idea to bring extra clothes on every rambling trip, as you never know when you'll be caught in a sudden downpour.

   Other than the appropriate clothes, you also need to bring the right type of footwear. There are many rambling trails where your average pair of sneakers just won't do.

3. A map of the area and if possible, of the trail itself. Obviously, you'll also need to have adequate map-reading skills. Many beginners in rambling get lost simply because they don't have a map or they don't really know how to read one.

   You should also have a detailed route plan based on your map. You have the option of drawing up your own route or securing one from a professional rambling source online.

4. A compass of good quality. Just like a map, you'll need at least some basic knowledge in using a compass as well. More importantly, you'll need to know how to use the compass in tandem with your map.

5. First aid kit. You don't have to bring a fancy and bulky kit. What's important is that your first aid kit has all the basic first aid tools necessary.

6. Pen and paper. It's always a good idea to take note of any memorable landmarks you come across for future reference. You may also want to keep a journal detailing your experience and the lessons you've gained from it, such as which things to avoid in the future or what items to add to your gear.

7. A wristwatch or any tool by which you can tell the time. This is very useful for tracking your speed and progress throughout the trip.

8. A ball of string. You'll be surprised at how useful this can be. In the same way, it's also a good idea to bring a Swiss army knife.

9. A whistle. This is very useful for emergencies where you need to call for help, especially when injuries are involved.

10. A flashlight. Even when you've just planned to spend a few hours on your rambling trip, you never know when you might get delayed and perhaps not be able to find your way back until nightfall.

Of course, you'll also need a sturdy backpack in which to carry all of the above. The good thing is that these things usually don't weight much even when put together.

What to Wear

Many people now treat outdoor recreation clothing as some sort of fashion statement.

But, you need to bear in mind that style shouldn't be the only consideration when you choose your clothes for an activity such as rambling.

Functionality and comfort should be among your most important considerations as well. Here are the most basic items of clothing you'll need for rambling:

1. A Waterproof Jacket

The jacket you choose for a rambling adventure should be able to effectively keep water out and shield you from the wind.

It's therefore a good idea to get a jacket with an outer shell made of waterproof material. It should also have the ability to let water vapour out, so you may want to check for breathability features.

Additionally, the jacket should have a hood that's big enough for you to pull up even when you have a hat on. It should also feature either a waterproof zipper or storm flaps over the zipper.

Finally, the jacket you choose should be big enough for you to wear comfortably over a few layers of clothing.

2. Inner Clothes

It's a much better idea to wear a few thin layers of clothing when going on a rambling trip than to wear just one thick layer. Layering allows you to adjust your clothing according to changes in temperatures and in your work load.

For example, you could shed a couple of layers as you start to go up a mountainside, which requires more exertion.

When you reach the top of the mountain, temperatures will likely drop, so you can put the two layers of clothing back on. Wool and synthetic materials are your best options for clothing. Try to avoid wearing cotton.

3. A Hat or Balaclava

Bear in mind that you lose a significant amount of heat from your head during winter. If you plan to go rambling at this time, then, you'll have to protect your head by wearing a hat or balaclava.

In the same way, the summer heat can cause overheating when you go rambling with your head exposed, so it's best to wear a hat at this time.

4. Gloves or Mittens

Your hands are among the parts of your body that are extremely difficult to keep warm and dry at the same time. This is especially true since a lot of the things you need to do can only be successfully done when you remove your mittens or gloves.

The best thing you can do where your hands are concerned is to wear a thin yet warm inner layer along with an outer layer made of waterproof material.

Take note that mittens are more effective than gloves in keeping your hands warm, but they also make some tasks more difficult to do.

And in case your gloves or mittens get wet, you may want to use a pair of sock temporarily as a substitute.

You may also need other items of clothing, depending on where you'll be rambling and for how long, as well as the time of year you're going on your trip.

However, the ones mentioned above are the most basic items you'll need and are must-haves no matter where, when, and for long you go rambling.

The Right Footwear

Ideally, you should go rambling with different footwear for the different conditions and terrains you're likely to encounter along the way.

But, that may not really be very practical for most ramblers and it is generally too expensive for a lot of people.

You will therefore have to choose a pair of boots that can perform well in a wide range of conditions and circumstances.

In most cases, you may have to choose between winter hiking boots that are designed for high-level walking and summer hiking boots that are designed for lower-level walking.

And just like almost anything else in life, you will likely get whatever you pay for in terms of quality, functionality, and longevity.

When you shop for a pair of rambling boots, you'll have to bear in mind the saying that boots can be compared to a good friend; they should offer support without being irritating.

Among the things you need to look for are waterproofing, sides that are high enough for adequate ankle support, and a good tread on the soles that's made from materials with excellent adhesive properties such as rubber.

It's advisable for you to avoid boots with PVC treads.

The heels and toe parts of your boots should also have extra strength for added protection, and the insoles and upper linings should be padded for a firm yet comfortable support for your feet.

Another thing you need to ensure is that the cuff – the section surrounding the top of your ankle – and the tongue of the boots are padded so as to keep water, stones, and debris from getting into your boots.

It's also a good idea to choose boots with hooks or D-rings instead of eyelets for the laces, since these are much easier for you to adjust even when your fingers are cold.

A locking hook also makes it easier for you to lace up. It would be best to buy your rambling boots from a shop specialising in outdoor activity equipment and gear, as they're likely to know exactly what you need.

You should also take your time when you fit and choose to make sure you get the right pair.

Don't forget to wear a pair of your rambling socks when you fit boots.

Take note that the right fit for your rambling boots is snug without being too tight. Remember that your feet are likely to become cold if you wear boots that are too tight. You should have the ability to freely wiggle your toes inside the boots, but they shouldn't touch the front part of the boots.

When you place a finger inside the boot at the back part, your toes should just touch the boot's front part.

You may also want to bear in mind that while general hill walking doesn't require soles that are particularly stiff, too much flexibility likely won't provide you with adequate feet protection.

When you go out shopping for rambling boots, don't hesitate to tell the boot specialist what type of walking you'll most likely be doing in your boots. This should give them a general idea of what type of boots you need.

What Food to Bring

There are a number of things to bring on a rambling adventure trip and food is just one of those things.

The value of bringing an adequate amount of food lies in the fact that it provides you with both physical and psychological benefits. These benefits become all the more significant when you go on rambling adventures uphill.

On the physical aspect, your body naturally gets energy from the food you eat whenever you move. The more strenuous your movements are, the more energy you need.

There are, of course, a number of factors that dictate the exact amount of energy that's needed for a particular activity such as rambling.

These factors include your age, your weight, your gender, the distance you'll be walking, and the elevation involved.

If you'll mostly be walking uphill, you'll need a considerable amount of carbohydrates and healthy fats.

You'll be forced to slow down if you don't get enough carbohydrates. Take note that healthy food intake also motivates you to complete your rambling expedition and enjoy the experience.

What's most important is for you to bring an adequate amount of water. Your body temperature is naturally controlled by sweating and if you fail to replenish the moisture that's lost when you sweat, you're likely to become dehydrated.

Dehydration can rapidly lead to heat exhaustion, so it's definitely important to take a drink of water from time to time as you keep walking and during every rest period.

Some people will tell you not to wait for a feeling of thirst before you drink water, but others recommend letting your thirst guide you as to when it's the right time to drink.

It would perhaps be best for you to drink water at the very first sign of thirst to make sure your water intake matches the rate of sweating.

This also allows you to prevent over-hydration, which leads to Hyponatraemia and affect all of your main organs.

Aside from water, you may also take drinks rich in electrolytes in order to manage your blood sodium levels, particularly when you're on a long rambling expedition.

Remember to bring food and drinks in adequate amounts so you don't become too exhausted as a result of a lack of energy. And because you'll be constantly on the move, you'll have to make sure the food you bring is light weight, while still providing the energy that you need.

Carbohydrate-rich food is your best option in this case. To illustrate, you may want bring two peanut butter or cheese sandwiches, a bar of chocolate, some peanuts, a cereal bar or dried fruit, and two litres of water for a day trip.

You may also want to note that the most effective way of consuming your food would be in small amounts several times throughout the day.

Before you go out for a rambling trip, you should also be sure to eat a good breakfast about an hour before your trip starts.

You'll also need to refuel within two hours of your trip's completion.

High-carbohydrate food is also ideal in this case. In case you sweated a lot during your adventure or if the trip was particularly long, then you should consider taking in saltier food as well.

Always remember that good nutrition is one of the keys to a successful rambling adventure.

Fitness for Rambling

Rambling is an outdoor adventure sport that requires both physical and mental efforts. In this section we look at the physical rigours you're likely to experience when you go rambling.

Additionally, we look at the basic fitness components you're going to need as well as some suggestions as regards how you can get started in building your fitness level for this outdoor activity.

It should come as no surprise that you'll need a certain level of fitness to successfully ramble regularly, especially if your expedition involves climbing up hills and mountains. There are several components of fitness that you can improve on with regular training.

These components include speed, strength, stamina, skill, flexibility, and even mental attitude.

A good combination of these individual aspects provides you with a solid foundation that allows you to truly enjoy the wonders of nature at levels that you're comfortable with.

When the amazing beauty of nature gets hold of you, you'll surely become addicted to outdoor activities like rambling, which involves a healthy combination of adventure and risk, thus being a truly exhilarating experience.

The basic fitness requirements for rambling may seem quite daunting for a beginner like you.

This is why you need to make sure you start properly and avoid doing too much at once. This is the first rule of fitness for rambling and you need to bear it in mind at all times.

Remember that rushing into things and overdoing your workouts will only cause unnecessary aches and pains too early in your rambling trip, thus wrecking your motivation.

The best way to start building your fitness level is with a good aerobic workout.

Among the best exercises to perform in this case are power walking, swimming, cycling, and running.

Your local rambling club may even offer programs that can get you started at this level.

Once you've built up your basic fitness level enough that you feel ready to work on the other aspects such as speed or strength, you may want to start thinking about going to a fitness facility or gym where you're likely to get assistance from fitness experts.

You may even check with nearby universities, as there are some sports departments that offer special fitness programs to the public.

If possible, work on your fitness along with a friend or with a group, so you'll always be motivated.

Exercising with a group also provides you with an excellent avenue to discuss and compare your fitness levels, your needs, and your goals, thus contributing to your progress.

Another thing you need to realize is that fitness not only benefits you while you're rambling. It also benefits you for the rest of your life.

Not only does it make your outdoor adventures a lot more manageable, but also enhances your physical and psychological well-being, thus allowing you to enjoy nature's beauty in its various forms for several years to come.

So, if you're serious about getting engaged in rambling and other outdoor activities, start working on improving your fitness levels now!

Safety Tips

Even when you'll only be rambling for a day, you'll need to ensure your safety throughout the trip.

The good news is that ensuring safety when rambling takes nothing more than common sense and proper planning.

Take note that even when the trail you're following isn't really part of the wilderness and more like a national park, there are still a number of ways by which you can get into trouble out there.

That's why it's still very important to take the necessary safety precautions.

Let's say you're out rambling solo on a hill just about ten miles from your home.

The day is pleasantly warm and the weather is good. The trail you're following is about 12 miles long and you expect to be back home before dark.

But then, as you step over a low hedge, you suddenly lose your footing and fall. In such a case, you'll be lucky if the only thing you hurt is your pride.

But, what if the fall is bad?

What if you broke your ankle?

Who's going to help you?

You may be just a few miles from the nearest residential area, but there's usually no one else around on a rambling trail.

This is especially true if you started your trip late and get into an accident at a time when most of the other ramblers in the area are already heading home.

The point we're trying to drive home is that you can get into trouble no matter what trail you're following and regardless of what time of year or day it is.

That's why you need to take note of at least the basic precautions for outdoor exploration activities like rambling.

The good thing about these precautions is that they're very easy to remember so you surely won't have a difficult time putting them all into practice.

1. Never go on a rambling trip alone. Although it can indeed be very relaxing to enjoy nature's beauty alone and enjoy some me time, walking solo in the wilderness is just begging for trouble.

2. Always share your rambling plans with a family member or friend and tell him when you expect to be back. It's also a good idea to leave your number with that person and get his number as well.

3. In case you suddenly change your plans in the middle of your expedition, be sure to let your anchor person know. It saves the other person from unnecessary worries in case you don't get back when he expects you to.

   At the same time, it assures you that there will always be someone who can call for help in case you get into trouble and don't get back in time.

4. When rambling in remote areas, be sure to bring the appropriate clothes, adequate amount of food and water, as well as a survival bag.

A survival bag is a large and sturdy plastic bag that can effectively shield you from the elements. It usually appears in a bright orange colour so as to be easily seen. It's lightweight and can easily be folded up and packed along with the rest of your gear.

The great outdoors is indeed exciting to explore and rambling is among the best activities for being one with nature.

You can increase your enjoyment of the outdoors even more by taking some simple yet necessary precautions such as those mentioned above.

Bear in mind that nature may be beautiful, but she often takes no prisoners!

Choosing a Route

Among the things that make such activities as rambling attractive is the fact that you can do it just about anywhere.

There are many people who don't really consider themselves dedicated ramblers, but they still walk nature trails on a regular basis, even if their walks simply involve strolling around the local park or following a short trail near their home.

If you prefer to walk down a more structured rambling trail, though, you can choose from among hundreds or perhaps even thousands of trails that can be categorized into the following:

1. National Trails

This category includes trails that have been recognized officially by the government and are managed by a corresponding government agency.

In Great Britain, national trails are among the most popular, frequently-traversed, and well-loved trails.

That may be because they cover areas that are truly beautiful and ramblers get to see plenty of amazing sights along the way.

National trails all over the world have been written about quite extensively and there are several guide books pertaining to them that can assist beginners like you.

2. Recreational Routes

Other than national parks, there are other nature trails you can ramble through. Although they may not be officially recognized by a government agency, many of these trails have been cleared by local authorities and created with the help of local rambler's clubs and organizations.

Even individual ramblers who don't really belong to any club often help in the creation and maintenance of new trails. These trails come in several different styles and distances. There are short health trails and long-distance endurance trails.

The one thing they have in common is that they're all way-marked with a distinct logo to help you ensure that you're on the correct route.

3. Long-distance Routes

As indicated by the category name, these are routes that usually take a few days to complete, as opposed to national trails, which typically cover shorter distances.

Most of these routes pass through areas where you'll experience nature's amazing beauty. The local authorities of each locality the trail goes through take part in the maintenance of the route.

Just like national trails and recreational trails, these routes are also way-marked with their own distinctive logos.

4. Unmarked Routes

These routes are often considered as hidden treasures by most ramblers. Although they aren't maintain by any government agency or non-government organization, some of these routes have been written about in books and magazines.

And though they haven't been officially recognized as trails, they've already caught the interest of many ramblers.

Perhaps the most well-known of these routes is the one that goes coast-to-coast in Northern England.

The route was originally conceived by a popular rambler and writer, Alfred Wainwright.

There are, of course, other rambling trails that may not have been written about just yet and you may even discover one near your place of residence.

Whether you choose to explore one of the trails you hear or read about, or go looking for a new one with your rambling buddies, you're sure to have a truly amazing experience as long as you taken all the necessary precautions.

Planning a Rambling Trip

A successful rambling trip doesn't just happen by accident. You'll have to plan it very carefully and consider a lot of factors to ensure it goes as smoothly and hassle-free as possible.

Among the first things you need to consider are the needs of everyone in your rambling group.

This means the rambling plan you prepare should suit every single member of the group.

This includes the type of terrain you'll be walking on, which should be comfortable enough for everyone in your group to complete. If you plan to bring your dogs on the trip, then you should consider their needs as well.

Another important consideration for a rambling adventure is the weather. Although the weather is bound to change at any time, it's a good idea for you to keep your eye on it so you'll have at least a general idea as regards the type of weather you'll have on the scheduled day of your trip.

Keep checking the weather forecasts until the actual morning of your rambling trip.

If there's any doubt at all about the weather, the rule is for you to reschedule it to a time when you're more certain of not being caught in adverse weather conditions.

Regardless of how long you've been planning for your outdoor adventure or how far the members of your rambling party had to travel to take part in the activity, it's still advisable to postpone it when you're unsure of the weather.

The inconvenience you experience is nothing when compared to the amount of risks you'll be taking by continuing on the trip in the middle of unpredictable weather conditions.

Bear in mind that safety should always be your utmost concern. The trail you plan to follow will still be there once the weather improves, so you can always reschedule your adventure to another time.

When you plan your rambling route, remember to get a decent estimate of how long it will take for you to complete the trip. Be sure to take into account the pace of the member of your group who walks the slowest.

Remember as well that your normal walking pace is affected by going both uphill and downhill, so you'll have to factor in the number of ascents and descents on the route as well.

Essentially, what you need to ensure is that your group can safely arrive at the end of the trail (for a day trip) or at the designated camp base (for trips that last more than a day) before the dark sets in.

Some rambling groups also plan activities such as photography and bird watching as part of their expedition. If you're doing the same, then you should factor those activities into the timing as well.

It's also important to check if there are special rules and restrictions in the area or permits that you need to secure before you set out. In some areas, you'll have to book your trip in advance so be sure to find out if this is necessary in your case.

Finally, you should make sure that you know how to use all of the items that you bring with you on the trip.

You may have all the necessary rambling gear, but they'll be useless unless you actually know the proper way of using them.

Planning your rambling adventure well allows for a more memorable and enjoyable outdoor experience.

Tips for Beginners

Some people get into rambling because they want to improve their health.

Some people engage in rambling because they want to manage their weight and keep fit.

Some people go rambling because they want to speed up their recovery from illness or injury.

Whatever your reason is for getting into this activity, it's definitely something that's worth your time.

One of the best things about rambling is that you can do it with your children or even with older members of your family.

People also appreciate the fact that it's significantly less expensive than other activities and it suits just about any lifestyle or domestic circumstance.

To successfully gain the health benefits of rambling and other activities that involve walking, you'll have to walk for a minimum of 30 minutes at a time at a pace that's as brisk as you can manage.

This means you need to walk fast enough that you won't be able to sing, but you can still comfortably carry a conversation.

If you have an existing medical condition, however, it's best to consult your doctor first before you go rambling so you'll know what types of trail you can safely follow and what your ideal walking speed is.

Try to include walking in your daily routine. This means taking a walk even when you're not going on a rambling trip. A 30-minute walk around the neighbourhood should do the trick.

It doesn't even matter what time of day you take your daily walk because you make the same effort regardless. It may help keep you motivated if you have a walking buddy.

For some people, keeping an activity journal is also a good motivator so you may want to try that as well.

If you want to compare the amount of walking you do from one day to the next, then you should get a pedometer. This could motivate you to take more rambling trips or at least walk more each day.

Whenever your plan a rambling trip, it's a good idea to set out for a short trip first and then gradually build up to longer and more challenging expeditions.

You may also want to note the amount of time it took you to complete the first route and then strive to shorten that time on a second trip before moving on to a longer route.

Remember not to push yourself too much and to avoid doing too much too soon. You gain the most benefits by building your strength and endurance gradually rather than working yourself to extreme exhaustion.

Never forget to warm up before setting out on a rambling adventure and then cool down right after.

If your expedition lasts for more than a day, then be sure to cool down before you rest for the night and then warm up again before setting out in the morning.

The best way to warm up is to do some stretching for at least five minutes and then start walking slowly for another five minutes.

You may then pick up your pace and lengthen your strides until you get to the point of brisk walking. In the same way, gradually reduce your pace and shorten your strides as you near your stopping point so you can properly cool down.

As soon as you stop, you'll have to do some stretching again before you finally rest. And as with any other physical activity, you'll have to keep yourself properly hydrated at all times.

Rambling Courses
for Beginners

There are several ways by which you can enjoy the benefits of rambling while learning some very important life skills at the same time.

Although you may encounter a number of pitfalls, it can be very satisfying to go the DIY route and learn from your very own experience.

Should you decide to go this route, however, you'll have to make sure that your rambling plans are always suited to your current fitness and experience level.

Try to achieve too much at once will only get you into trouble and may even lead to some serious and life-threatening consequences.

There are many people who believe that it's very dangerous to go on rambling adventures alone.

For some people, however, solo rambling is one of life's greatest pleasures. If you choose to go solo, though, you'll have to make sure you're experienced and skilled enough so you don't put yourself at an unnecessary risk.

Being able to ensure your own safety is crucial to ensuring your enjoyment of the activity and the beauty of nature as well.

More often than not, the best way to start in any activity or sport is by trying it out with friends. This is true as well of rambling. If you're lucky enough to know some ramblers, then you could go on one of their rambling trips to begin with.

Make sure you tell your friends this is your first time out so they don't take you on a trail that's too much for you to handle.

Take note that if you choose to get into rambling simply by starting out with friends, you can't expect to get a structured or formal training as regards the necessary skills for the activity.

If you want some formal instruction in this exciting outdoor adventure, then you'll have to take a course. In this course, you can expect to learn about the different aspects of rambling and a lot of other things you may not even have considered when you started going on rambling trips with your friends.

Among other things, you'll learn the value of proper pacing, different ways of saving your energy, how to respond to emergencies, map-reading and compass use, and the most important things to bring with you on a rambling trip.

There are numerous courses on rambling being offered all over the world. What you need to look for is a course that's being offered by a qualified and reputable rambling expert.

Take note that the basic qualification for ramblers is a Walking Group Leader's Certificate.

While this allows a person to lead others on a rambling trip over low hills and safer trails, this doesn't give him license to teach rambling skills.

The qualification you need to look for in a rambling instructor is a Mountaineering Instructor's Award, which is the most basic qualification that allows a person to both lead and teach.

Someone with a Mountaineering Instructor's Certificate can instruct even for winter rambling.

While it isn't really necessary for you to get formal instruction in order to get into rambling, it provides a lot of benefits in terms of basic knowledge and skills.

This is especially true if you've never walked in the wilderness before.

What to Do When
You Get Lost

No matter how much preparation you do before you go on a rambling adventure, there are just times when you somehow become lost in the wilderness.

Your preparation may have helped ensure that you have the ability to find your way back to the trail, but the most important thing you need to bear in mind is that you shouldn't panic.

Many ramblers continue walking blindly when they realize they've gotten lost simply because they panic and begin to think that if they just go on, they'll soon come across a familiar landmark.

What you need to do instead is stop as soon as you realize that you're lost.

Once you've stopped, take a deep breath and then find a good place to sit down so you can think things through.

This is also a good time for you to drink some water and have some food while assessing the situation and gathering your thoughts.

Try to recall the last time you were still sure of your exact location and then think about the waypoints or landmarks you've just passed, which you may be able to identify on your map.

Once you've identified the nearest landmark or waypoint, navigate your way towards that location. Repeat the process until you find yourself back on the trail.

If you're rambling with a group, then it is best to discuss your options with the other members of your rambling party.

Every person has a different observation when walking amidst the beauty of nature. Someone in your group may have seen an important landmark the rest of you may have overlooked.

It may also be a good idea to ask everyone to just be still for a minute and just listen to the sounds around you.

Sound often triggers off memories of the things you saw along the way and these memories may just get you back on track.

As you try to make your way to the last landmark you remember, you may let out whistle or shout for help from time to time. You may be closer to other people than you realize.

Even if a member of your group says he's confident that he can guide you back to safety, you should still assess your current situation properly.

Among the things you need to consider are the weather conditions and the time of day.

If there's even the slightest doubt that you'll be able to reach the familiar landmark in time due to inclement weather or because it's almost dark, it would be better for you to just find a good place to set up camp for the night and then resume your assessment in the morning.

Taking time to rest could also refresh your memory and make it easier for you to recall waypoints and landmarks.

GPS devices and mobile phones will obviously be very helpful in situations where you become lost in the wilderness.

Other than this, however, there are several ways by which you can summon help.

You could find a clear area where you'll be more visible to other people or rescue teams that may already be looking for you. It's also a good idea to build a signal fire in this area.

Make sure the smoke you generate is big enough to be noticed from above, in case rescuers in a helicopter are out looking for your group.

Whatever assessment you come up with and whatever steps you decide to make when you're lost in the great outdoors, the most important tip is still this: don't panic.

Why Join a Rambling Club?

You know how refreshing it is to be out there savouring the feeling of being one with nature and challenging yourself to cover greater distances and achieve greater heights as you wonder at nature's beauty.

Take note, however, you often need to properly organize your rambling adventure in order to truly enjoy the experience.

Should you choose to go solo, you'll have to plan where you'll be going, what specific route you'll be taking, what you're going to bring, and where you'll camp for the night, among other things.

As a beginner in this outdoor adventure sport, you'd do well to join a rambling club. Such organizations usually allow you to go on a rambling trip or two so you can decide whether you and the club are a good fit and of it's a good idea to become a permanent member.

Regardless of what your current fitness level is, a rambling club will surely be able to design a trip that suits you well.

You'll also be grouped with other beginners within the same fitness levels and you'll have an experienced leader who can properly introduce you to every aspect of a rambling expedition.

One of the best things about joining a rambling club is that their expeditions are well-organized and the club itself is likely to have a listing of the world's best rambling routes for you to explore.

It's easy enough to find a rambling club within your locality. You could ask family members and friends who've gone rambling before if they know of any rambling club in your area.

You may also want to check your Yellow Pages for a listing of local rambling clubs.

Additionally, you do a simple online search to see if there any rambling clubs near you. There are rambling clubs with just a few members and there are also those with a great number of members.

What these clubs have in common is that they typically have regular meetings for planning, for actual expeditions, or simply for socialising and getting to know each other.

Rambling clubs are organized such that expeditions are graded differently. You may then choose a specific grade, which you feel is best suited to your fitness and skill level.

Needless to say, the different grades correspond to the level of difficulty or challenge presented by the route as well as the distance covered. Of course, joining a rambling club isn't a requirement for you to enjoy this activity.

You can go rambling by yourself or with a group of friends. After all, a hike is something anyone can enjoy in whatever way they like.

Joining a club, however, is a sure way of enjoying the activity while ensuring your safety in the company of experienced ramblers.

20970721R00059

Printed in Great Britain
by Amazon